Star Poems

Compiled by John Foster

OXFORD

Oxford University Press, Great Clarendon Street,
Oxford OX2 6DP

Oxford New York
Athens Auckland Bangkok Bogotá Buenos Aires
Calcutta Cape Town Chennai Dar es Salaam
Delhi Florence Hong Kong Istanbul Karachi
Kuala Lumpur Madrid Melbourne Mexico City
Mumbai Nairobi Paris São Paulo Singapore
Taipei Tokyo Toronto Warsaw

and associated companies in
Berlin Ibadan

Oxford is a trade mark of Oxford University Press

First published 1993
Reprinted 1995, 1996, 1998, 1999
ISBN 0 19 916599 8
Printed in Hong Kong

A CIP Catalogue record for this book is available from the British Library

Acknowledgements
The Editor and Publisher wish to thank the following who have kindly given permission for the use of copyright materials:

Moira Andrew for 'Star shapes' and 'The Christmas star' both ©1991 Moira Andrew; Tony Bradman for 'The sun', 'My telescope' and 'Shooting star' all ©1991 Tony Bradman; Mary Dawson for 'Spinning stars' ©1991 Mary Dawson; Eric Finney for 'How to draw a hexagram' ©1991 Eric Finney; John Foster for 'On a starry night' ©1991 John Foster; Clive Riche for 'Star fish' ©1991 Clive Riche.

Although every effort has been made to contact the owners of copyright material, a few have been impossible to trace, but if they contact the Publisher correct acknowledgement will be made in future editions.

Illustrations by
Jan Lewis, Caroline Jayne Church, Gill Scriven, Valerie McBride, Christine Blaney, Andy Cooke, Rhian Nest James, Louise Metcalf.

The sun

The wind is whistling.
The sky is grey.
You're off to school
On a miserable day.

Clouds are pouring
Rain on your head.
You wish you could
Have stayed in bed.

But 92 million
Miles from here
Is a star that will make
Your gloom disappear.

Its rays will cross
The deeps of space
To make you smile
When they touch your face.

The sun will chase
Your blues away.
For who can be sad
On a bright, sunny day?

Tony Bradman

My telescope

I bought myself a telescope
To look into the sky
To see the solar system
And the comets whizzing by.

I search the sky for planets,
For satellites and stars,
And now I've got a telescope
They don't seem very far.

It's brought them very close to me,
It's made the stars my friends . . .
Except, of course, when I make a mistake
And look through the wrong end!

Tony Bradman

On a starry night

On a starry night
The stars twinkle
Like thousands of bright eyes
Watching us and winking.

On a cloudy night
The stars are hidden
As if someone
Has blindfolded them.

John Foster

Shooting star

Shooting star
Burning bright
In the middle
Of the night

Zooming through
The galaxy
On your way
To me, to me.

I'll wish a wish
Before you die
And tumble down
The starry sky

That once again
One magic night
I might see you
Burning bright.

Tony Bradman

The Christmas star

A star looked down
from the frosty sky,
saw three lost Kings
and winked its eye.

'Follow me,' it said
and blazed a trail
over sand and plain,
up-hill, down-dale.

It stopped at Bethlehem
above a poor shed.
'Here?' asked the Kings.
'The Child has no bed.'

'Here,' said the star
and faded from sight,
as sun bathed the Baby
in clear morning light.

Moira Andrew

Spinning stars

Oh! What fun it must be to feel
You're whirling round like a Catherine Wheel.
Slowly at first as it circles round
Scattering stars all over the ground.
Then faster and faster it spins and soon
The fiery ball's like a big round moon.

Now the stars have vanished
The moon's a ghost . . .
And . . . all . . . that's left . . .
Is . . . the . . . pin
In . . . the . . . post.

Mary Dawson

How to draw a hexagram

Start with a triangle –
A shape of great strength –
A point at the top,
Three sides the same length.
All O.K. so far?
Call this triangle one.

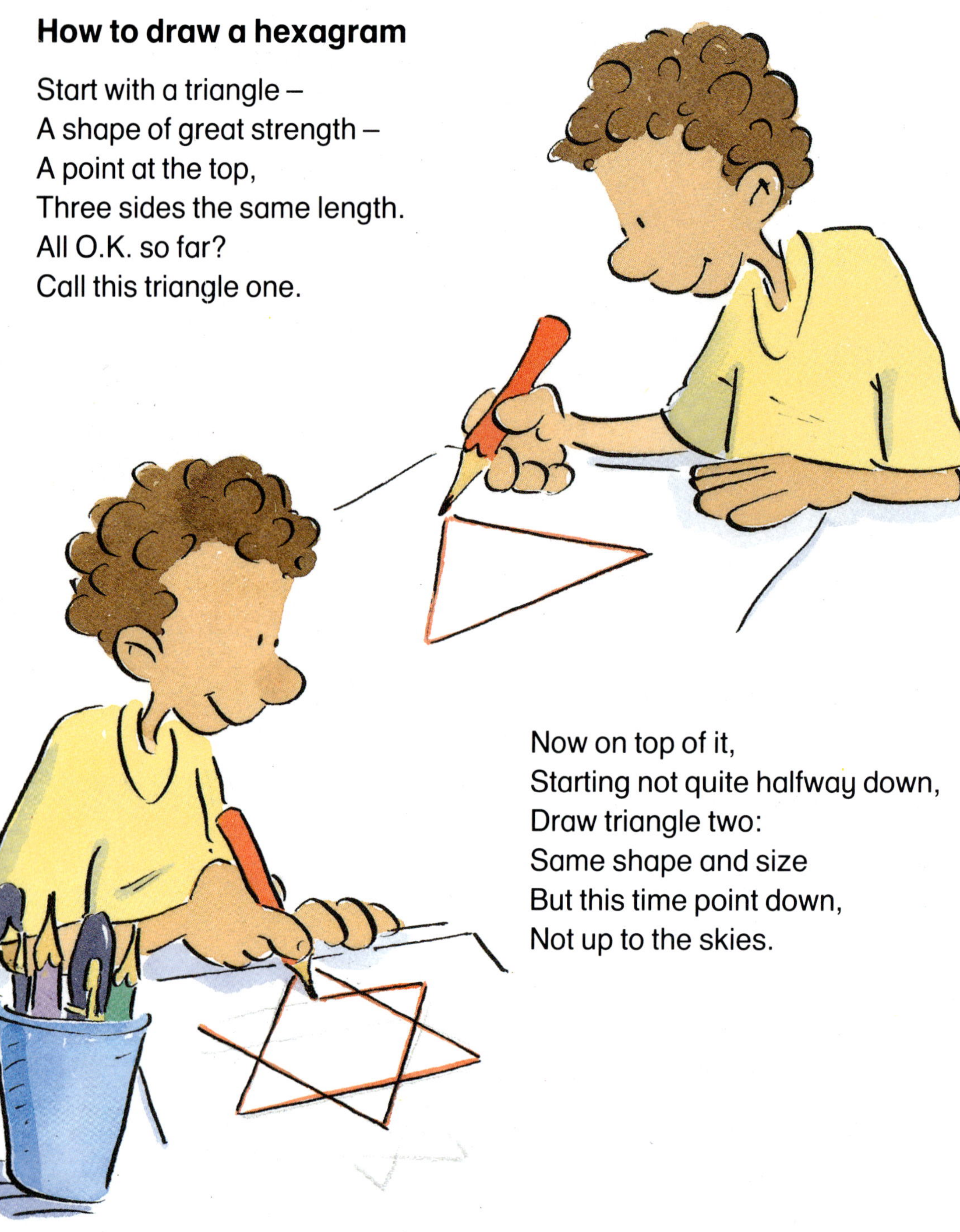

Now on top of it,
Starting not quite halfway down,
Draw triangle two:
Same shape and size
But this time point down,
Not up to the skies.

It’s a six-pointed star:
How clever you are!
You’ll be tired after that,
But don’t stretch and yawn:
Instead find out
How many triangles you’ve drawn.

Eric Finney

Star fish

Star fish Star fish
Sparkling white,
Did you fall out of the night?
Were you once a star above,
Come to see the earth you love?
To see the people here below
To let them touch you, so they know,
That there are stars inside the sea
That stars are just like you and me,
That there are stars along the beach
Beneath our feet, within our reach?
Star fish Star fish
Sparkling white
Did you fall out of the night?

Clive Riche

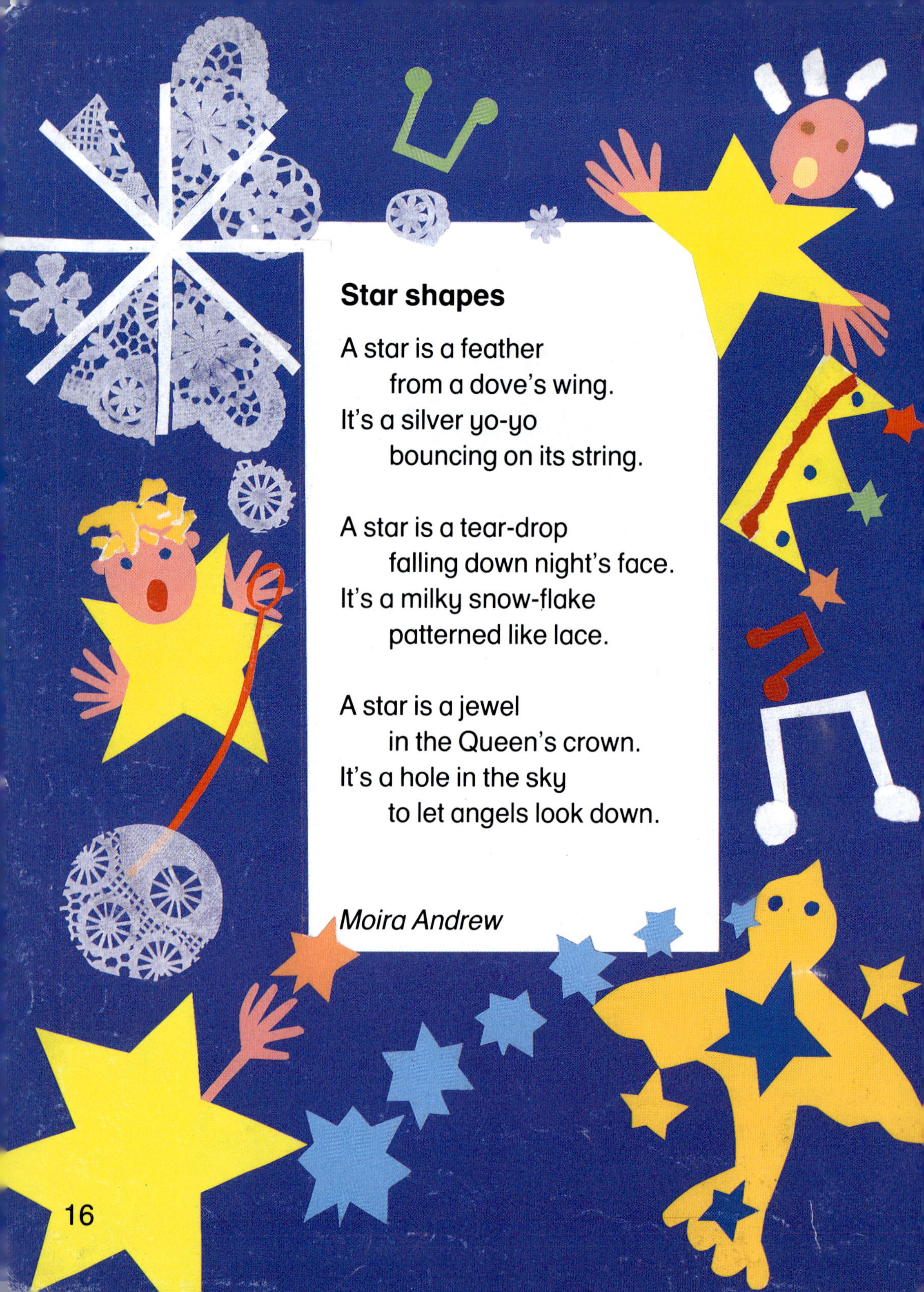

Star shapes

A star is a feather
    from a dove's wing.
It's a silver yo-yo
    bouncing on its string.

A star is a tear-drop
    falling down night's face.
It's a milky snow-flake
    patterned like lace.

A star is a jewel
    in the Queen's crown.
It's a hole in the sky
    to let angels look down.

Moira Andrew